Should

PSAL*

be the

ONLY HYMNAL

of the Church?

Iain H. Murray

THE BANNER OF TRUTH TRUST

THE BANNER OF TRUTH TRUST
3 Murrayfield Road, Edinburgh EH12 6EL, UK
P.O. Box 621, Carlisle, PA 17013, USA

✻

© Iain H. Murray 2001

ISBN 0 85151 809 5

✻

Typeset in 11/13 pt Sabon MT
Printed in Great Britain by
Howie & Seath,
Edinburgh

Should the Psalter Be the Only Hymnal of the Church?

Common Ground

1. Praise is to be addressed to God alone. 'Singing . . . to the Lord' (*Eph*. 5:19). Where the attitude of worshippers is not in accord with this fact, the name of God is being taken in vain.

2. Though owed by all men, praise can only be truly offered by Christians for it requires the aid of the Holy Spirit. 'Be filled with the Spirit . . . singing' (*Eph*. 5:18–19).

3. The content of praise must be such as is appropriate to the worshipper and therefore capable of being spoken from the heart in sincerity and in accord with the reality of his own experience.

4. To be honouring to God, and capable of being sung by believers in faith, the substance of praise must be controlled by biblical truth (*Matt*. 15:9).

5. The singing of praise, as well as being to the glory of God, is intended to be of special benefit to believers in the uplifting of their spirits. Poetry is the language of emotion. Joyless singing is a contradiction. 'The duty of singing praises to God seems to be appointed wholly to excite and

express religious affections . . . No other reason can be assigned why we shall express ourselves to God in verse rather than in prose.'[1] 'The lively voice does not only give vent to affections, but increases them . . . Besides this [there is] the benefit we may convey to others by loud singing; one bird sets the whole flock a-chirping. Augustine speaketh how much he was moved by the melody and singing of the church at Milan.'[2]

6. It has also to be recognised that there is a human element necessarily involved in this discussion. Things which have become part of our lives are not readily changed. Tunes associated with all the memories of childhood are likely to be with us all our days and their use or disuse belongs to those issues 'common to human actions and societies, which are to be ordered by the light of nature and Christian prudence' (*Westminster Confession* I:6). Whether, for instance, psalms should be chanted (as the practice of the Eastern and other Churches) or sung in metrical form is scarcely a matter of principle and such things are usually determined by custom.

THE AREA OF CONTROVERSY

For congregational praise there clearly needs to be a book or books for common use. The one question which I want to address is whether or not Christians and churches are left to form their own judgment on the material they use for this purpose, or whether there is a principle which requires them

---

[1] Jonathan Edwards, *Works* (repr. Edinburgh: Banner of Truth, 1974), vol. 1, p. 242; vol. 2, p. 917.

[2] Thomas Manton, *Complete Works* (London: Nisbet, 1871), vol. 4, p. 444.

to use one book alone, namely the Book of Psalms (that is, the Psalter in metrical form). It needs to be noted that there would be no controversy here if the question is simply whether we find hymns or metrical psalms more helpful. If it is only a question of preference and not of principle then we are not likely to want to dispute with other Christians or to urge them to change their present practice. But a serious difference does arise when, as in recent publications,[3] it is urged that Christians are not at liberty to determine what they shall sing in public worship. This view is based on the belief that the Psalter is divinely appointed for singing and that, if we sing anything else, then we are disobeying the requirements of Scripture.

THE PSALMS-ONLY CASE STATED

'The Bible contains one book of praise, the Psalms. It is the inspired Word of God and the Spirit of God, its author, possessed the knowledge to make it appropriate for the use of the church in all ages. Further, God claims in Scripture the right to determine how he shall be worshipped (see *Westminster Confession*, XXI), and if this "regulative principle" be applied to praise, as it ought to be, then we should use no book other than the one he has given to us. "Could not the Lord then give what would be suitable for all

---

[3] A number have appeared. They include: F. J. Smith and D. C. Lachman, *Worship in the Presence of God* (Greenville, S.C., 1992); *The Psalms in Worship*, ed. J. McNaugher (Pittsburgh, 1907; repr. Edmonton: Still Waters Revival Books, 1992); John Murray and William Young, *The Scriptural Warrant respecting Song in the Public Worship of God* (repr. Vienna, Va.: Presbyterian Reformed Church, 1993); John W. Keddie, *Sing the Lord's Song: Biblical Psalms in Worship* (Edinburgh: Knox Press, 1994).

ages? Can uninspired men now do better than he did then?" What possible justification, therefore, can there be for substituting human compositions, however good, for the inspired praises of the Psalter? When we have the very Psalms which Christ himself sang in praise who can consciously choose to sing something else? In the words of Bishop Wordsworth: "The Psalter has no echo in the New Testament. It belongs to both Testaments. It speaks of Christ and Christ speaks in it. It is the hymn-book of the universal church."'

Such is the argument, briefly stated. And lest it should be supposed by anyone that psalm-singing passed away in the New Testament era, an appeal can be made to history to show that the practice was general in the churches throughout many centuries. It was universal in the Calvinistic churches of the Reformation, and the Puritans, Huguenots, Scots Covenanters, Welsh Calvinistic Methodists, and many more, were psalm-singers.

This argument looks impressive to anyone who takes the Bible seriously and, if the case is true that inspired material for the praise of the churches in all ages is alone warranted by Scripture, then loyalty to the truth would require the disuse of all hymnody in public worship. A principle is thus involved in this discussion and one that is necessarily controversial for those who sing hymns.

A RESPONSE

In responding to what is claimed, it is essential to distinguish different issues. The issue is not how highly do we regard the Book of Psalms. C. H. Spurgeon spent more than twenty years in expounding the Psalms in the six volumes of his *Treasury of David*, and he could say at the end, 'Can I hope to spend hours more joyous on this side of the golden gate?' But he had no hesitation about compiling and using a hymn book.[4] Nor is the issue whether or not psalms should be sung (we believe they should); it is whether they should be sung exclusively. In response to the exclusive claim I offer the following observations:

1. *Where is the proof in Scripture that God appointed the one-hundred-and-fifty Psalms of David for the public worship of the Old Testament church?*

That some fifty-five Psalms were given to be sung by Levitical choirs in public worship, perhaps with responses from the general congregation, is not questioned. But the title of other Psalms, such as the seventeenth and the ninetieth, refers to them as prayers, indeed a section of the Book appears to have been given that name at the end of Psalm 72: 'The prayers of David the son of Jesse are ended.' Other Psalms, perhaps forty in number, may be said to be chiefly for instruction. That all the Psalms were ever used in the temple in worship, or that all were ever given for congregational praise, is simply an assumption and rests on no evidence. For many Psalms there is no indication at all that they were to be set to music for public worship. Such a committed psalm-singer as William Binnie concedes this point. Referring to the Book of Psalms, he writes:

'The greater number are of a kind little suited to the splendid mode of performance characteristic of the temple. I will not affirm that the Hundred and nineteenth Psalm, for

---

[4] For Spurgeon's disagreement with exclusive psalmody see his review of *The True Psalmody; or, The Bible Psalms the Church's Only Manual of Praise*, in *The Sword and the Trowel*, 1889, p. 237.

example, was never sung by the Levitical choirs: but the likelihood is, that it never was.'[5]

Even the fact that Scripture designates a part of Scripture as a 'song'(*shir*) is not itself proof that it is necessarily given for public worship. For if that were the case then the book (The Song of Solomon) which the Holy Spirit describes as 'the song of songs' – that is, the most superlative of songs – ought to have first place in congregational praise. To argue that because we have only one inspired 'Book of Praises', therefore nothing of merely human composition is ever to be set to music for the praise of God, is thus to make a deduction which goes beyond anything which Scripture actually says.

Nowhere in Scripture is the idea presented that praise *spoken* has to be restricted to Bible words, words appointed by the Holy Spirit; why then should praise *sung* be different? Further, as already said, the Book of Psalms contains many prayers. It could be called a Book of Prayers as well as a Book of Praises. In that respect there is nothing comparable to it elsewhere in Scripture, yet no one holds that the prayers of the church must ever be restricted to the inspired words that God has given us.

If the exclusive argument were true it would mean there is a prohibition concerning sung praise which is in marked contrast with the freedom believers have in expressing all desires and thanksgivings which are not set to music. On this point Robert S. Candlish has written: 'There is as much prayer as praise in the Psalms. I see no room whatever for saying that the Psalms is purely a psalmodical book. It contains prayers as well as praises . . . I cannot understand

[5] William Binnie, *The Psalms: Their History, Teaching and Use* (London: Nelson, 1870), p. 360.

how we should be more hampered and fettered as regards the use of our words in the one part of divine worship than in the other.'[6]

The point I have just made is countered by saying that in ascribing public praise to God in song we need to have an accuracy of speech which can be found only in words of divine inspiration. But this is again assuming what cannot be proved. It might equally be argued that the preaching of the Word of God to dying men and women requires an accuracy of speech beyond all human abilities and that preachers should therefore be restricted to the very words of Scripture and to no other. To say that the Book of Psalms gives us wonderful examples of how God is to be praised is one thing, to say that the whole Psalter and nothing else is intended for public worship is another.

James Hamilton summarised what I am saying in these words:

'The great magazine of devotional materials I believe to be the Word of God, and for such purposes the portion pre-eminent I believe to be the book of Psalms; but believing, as I do, that not even the Jew was bound to pray or sing in words wholly Biblical, I can far less believe that Christ has left His people under any such bondage.'[7]

2. As said above, poetry is the language of emotion. Hebrew poetry, however, is very different from our own. It is in prose not metre and, if keeping as close as possible to the exact

---

[6] W. Wilson, *Memorials of R. S. Candlish* (Edinburgh: Black, 1880), p. 544. Candlish, in the opinion of Dr Gordon, was 'pre-eminently the preacher of the Free Church of Scotland'. His words, quoted above, were given in the context of his statement, 'I want some hymns.'

[7] James Hamilton, *The Psalter and the Hymn Book: Three Lectures* (London: Nisbet, 1865), pp. 18–19.

words is required of us, then there has to be a strong case for saying that the Churches which chanted the psalms were more correct. It is hard to see how chanting would be musically uplifting in congregational praise today. In order to put Hebrew into metre in English some freedom needs to be used, but the question of how much freedom is permissible again comes back to the issue of whether it is the words of the Psalms, and those words only, to which we are tied. (For a contrast in the degree of freedom used by versifiers of the Psalms, compare Psalm 80 in the Scots and Irish versions with the beautiful version of the same Psalm, *Great Shepherd Who leadest Thy people in love,* in the American United Presbyterian *Psalter.*[8])

3. *If it could be proved that the Psalter alone was the authorised praise of the Old Testament church, it would still be another proposition altogether to establish that it must remain the sole manual for the New.*

The case that it does so remain rests on:

i. The so-called 'regulative principle', namely that what God has not appointed he has forbidden, and God has not appointed any second hymnal to supplement the Psalter. I will return to this point shortly.

ii. Alleged New Testament evidence. It is said that the 'psalms, hymns and spiritual songs' of Ephesians 5:19 refer solely to different sections of the Old Testament Psalter. We know of no prominent orthodox commentator who takes that view (see J. Eadie, C. Hodge, R.C.H. Lenski, W. Hendriksen, etc.). Eadie, for example says: 'As a considerable portion of the church at Ephesus was composed of Jews, these psalms in the idiom of the Jew might be the Psalms of

---

[8] *The Psalter* (repr. Grand Rapids: Eerdmans, 1977), pp. 188–9.

the Old Testament . . . and the hymns might be the compositions of praise specially adapted to the Gentile mind, though not inappropriate to the Jew. The imagery, allusions, and typical references of the Psalms could not be fully appreciated by the Gentile sections of the churches.'[9]

If the material of the praise referred to in Ephesians 5:19 is uncertain, it is far less so in the case of 1 Corinthians 14:26, 'Every one of you hath a psalm.' It appears to mean, says Hodge, 'such a song given by inspiration, and not one of the Psalms of David.' Even such a leading psalm-singer as John Cotton agrees with Hodge.[10]

THE REGULATIVE PRINCIPLE

This principle, with the corollary that it excludes all praise not divinely authorised, lies at the heart of the case for exclusive psalmody. Hymnody, it is said, is supplanting the Word of God by the words of men.

To this we have already replied that Scripture does not command any one manual of praise for the exclusive use of the church. The regulative principle controls what shall or shall not be parts of worship: it is sung praise that is authorised as a part, not the very words of which that part has to be made up. But to this it is commonly objected by exclusive psalm-singers that the best Reformed churches and authors thought otherwise and saw hymns of human composure as an intrusion on divine authority.

[9] John Eadie, *Commentary on the Greek Text of the Epistle to the Ephesians* (Edinburgh, 1883), p. 401.

[10] C. Hodge, *Commentary on Ephesians* (London: Banner of Truth, 1964), p. 304; John Cotton, *Singing of Psalms a Gospel Ordinance* (London; 1650), pp. 32–3.

On the contrary, I believe it can be shown that the use of the Psalter in the Reformed Churches was not generally based on the restriction which more modern writers have claimed to find in the regulative principle. Indeed the application of that principle to material other than psalms was perhaps unknown to the reformers. It was certainly unknown to Luther and Louis F. Benson writes, 'Even at Geneva, the fountain head of Metrical Psalmody, the addiction to psalms was not exclusive – no divine prescription was claimed for the Psalter. Calvin's *Genevan Psalter* included as a matter of fact such materials as the Commandments and Nunc Dimittis.'[11] Other material to be found in the same *Genevan Psalter* included a hymn, which has been attributed to Calvin, *Je te salue, mon certain Redempteur* ('I greet thee, who my sure Redeemer art').[12] Whether this fine hymn be Calvin's composition or not, it has been repeatedly attributed to the Psalter of his day. The priority he gave to psalms was by way of preference, not principle.

When the Reformation began in Scotland it is also clear that there were no objections to songs which were more paraphrases than translations of the psalms remaining as

[11] Louis F. Benson, *The English Hymn: Its Development and Use In Worship* (New York: Hodder and Stoughton, 1915), pp. 27, 55. Benson's work first appeared in the pages of the *Princeton Theological Review*.

[12] The hymn, from 1560, was included in the sixth volume of the *Works of Calvin*, edited by Baum, Cunitz, and Reuss, 1868, and, translated by David Bannerman. It was republished in P. Schaff and Arthur Gilman, *A Library of Religious Poetry* (New York: Funk and Wagnalls, 1880), pp. 610–11. *Trinity Hymnal* (OPC: Philadelphia, 1961) attributes a different translation of the same hymn to the *Strasbourg Psalter,* 1545, and the *Genevan Psalter,* 1551. Julian's *Dictionary of Hymnology* (London: J. Murray, 1892) also says the hymn first appeared in the *Strasbourg Psalter* of 1545.

closely as possible to the original.[13] The Scots Psalter of 1564, which remained in general use to the time of the Westminster Assembly, was based largely on the work of Sternhold and Hopkins and while their renderings usually kept closer to the original than paraphrases, they were clearly not composed in the conviction that nothing other than the biblical text may be introduced.[14]

Again, no school of men were stronger on what is called the regulative principle than were the English and Scottish Puritans, and yet, with the exception of John Cotton, we know of none who believed that biblical principle debarred the use of hymns. John Ball, for instance, the English Puritan leader, whose *Catechism* prepared the way for the *Shorter Catechism*, and who would have been at the Westminster Assembly had he not died in 1640 at the age of fifty-five, speaks directly to the issue. In a discussion in which he defends the use of written prayers, the ground he takes demonstrates that there was no controversy among them whether God allows praise other than the Book of Psalms to be sung in the churches. From the freedom allowed in song he argued a similar freedom over public prayer:

'For the psalms penned by the prophets are patterns and forms of spiritual songs, but not the set forms prescribed to us as psalms to be sung in those very words and forms. Though the psalms be parts of the canonical scripture, our brethren must esteem the use of them as a prescript form to

---

[13] See for instance the words sung by George Wishart at his martyrdom, as given in *Scots Worthies*.

[14] In the new version of the 1640s, says Robert Baillie, there was a 'resolving to keep punctuallie to the original text'. Quoted in Millar Patrick, *Four Centuries of Scottish Psalmody* (London: OUP, 1949), p. 54.

be the devise of man; because God has not given them to that end, nor by his commandment tied us and all churches to them and none others, in the precise form of words. When in the New Testament we are exhorted to sing psalms, they will not say that we are tied to David's psalms, or other songs given by immediate inspiration . . . In the New Testament since Christ we have no precedent of any stinted form of singing.'[15]

Another Puritan leader, Thomas Manton, who wrote the 'Epistle to the Reader' commonly found printed with the Westminster Confession, took a similar position to Calvin in his preference for the Psalter, but he likewise knew nothing of any principle debarring the use of any other praise: 'I confess we do not forbid other songs; if grave and pious, after good advice they may be received into the Church. Tertullian, in his *Apology,* showeth that in the primitive times they used this liberty, either to sing scripture psalms or such as were of private composure.'[16]

---

[15] John Ball, *A Friendly Trial of the Grounds Tending to Separation* (London: 1640), pp. 58–9. Baxter said that Ball 'deserved as high esteem and honour as the best bishop in England', yet he was silenced for nonconformity. Next to his *Catechism* (nineteenth impression, 1642), his books (especially on *Faith* and on *The Covenant of Grace*) were widely read. See the commendation of A. B. Grosart in his 'Memoir of Richard Sibbes', *Complete Works of Richard Sibbes*, vol. 1 (Edinburgh: Nichol, 1862), p. ci.

[16] Thomas Manton, *Complete Works*, vol. 4, p. 444. I am not in these pages entering into the evidence of the correctness of what Manton states on 'the liberty of the church in primitive times', except to say that long before Tertullian, within ten years of the death of the apostle John, a Roman governor, Pliny, is to be found describing Christians as those who 'assemble early in the morning, and sing among themselves alternately a hymn to Christ as to God.' See also the quotation from Joseph Bingham on p. 32.

No one was a stronger upholder of the regulative principle than John Flavel. We find him writing: 'Men cannot invent a surer and speedier way to their own ruin, than to bring their own inventions into God's worship.' But far from supposing that hymns belonged to that category he provides 'A Hymn' of his own composition in the same volume in which the warning was written.[17]

David Dickson, the Scots Puritan leader, likewise wrote hymns 'to be sung with any common tunes of the Psalms.'[18] How prevalent some of his hymns were in Scotland may be judged from an incident which occurred many years later in America. The story is told of a Scottish soldier who lay dying in New Orleans, and resisting all the spiritual conversation of a Presbyterian minister who sought to care for him. On the minister's second visit the man turned his face to the wall 'as if determined to hear nothing and relent nothing.

The minister bethought himself, as a last resource, of the hymn well known in Scotland, the composition of David Dickson, minister of Irvine, beginning, *O mother dear, Jerusalem, when shall I come to thee?*, which his Scottish mother had taught him to sing to the tune "Dundee". He began to sing his mother's hymn. The soldier listened for a few moments in silence, but gradually turned himself round, with a relaxed countenance, and the tear in his eye, to inquire, "Wha learned ye that?" "My mother", replied the minister. "And so did mine", rejoined

---

[17] *Works of John Flavel*, vol. 6 (London: Baynes, 1820), pp. 13, 469–70.

[18] 'True Christian Love', appended to Dickson's, *Truth's Victory over Error* (Glasgow, 1764).

the now softened soldier, whose heart was opened by the recollection of infancy and country.'[19]

Some of Dickson's verse is as worthy as Richard Baxter's to be sung today. My point in these quotations, however, is to indicate that in the seventeenth century the idea that sung praise must be confined to the Psalter was so unknown that Puritans saw no need to justify their words or verses. The same is true of the best-known successor to the Puritans, Jonathan Edwards who has sometimes been mistakenly claimed as an exclusive psalm-singer. In fact, Edwards wrote that while he was 'far from thinking that the Book of Psalms should be thrown by in our public worship . . . I know of no obligation we are under to confine ourselves to it.'[20] When hymns were introduced into his Northampton church during the Great Awakening, opposition in the congregation seems to have centred on one individual who claimed the support of the Rev. Benjamin Colman of Boston. Edwards seemed to find this claim unbelievable and wrote to Colman, 'I was ready to think there was some mistake, and it is pity that trouble should arise among us from nothing.'[21]

---

[19] The anecdote is printed after Dickson's hymn, *'The New Jerusalem; or, the Soul's Breathing after her Heavenly Country'* in *Tracts on the Doctrine, Order and Polity of the Presbyterian Church in the United States of America*, vol. 7 (Philadelphia: Presbyterian Board, n.d.[1835?]). The hymn is actually Dickson's rendering of a composition of earlier date. See *Trinity Hymnal* (1961), 603.

[20] Edwards, *Works*, vol. 1 (repr. Edinburgh: Banner of Truth, 1974), p. 396.

[21] Edwards, *Letters and Personal Writings*, ed. George S. Claghorn (New Haven: Yale University Press: 1998), pp. 144–5. He told his Boston friend how hymn-singing began in his congregation while he was away from home: ' I saw in the people a very general inclination to it – and seemed to be greatly pleased with it; and sang nothing else, and neglected the Psalms wholly. When I came home I disliked not their making use of the hymns, but did not like their setting aside the Psalms.'

Even in the Scottish Presbyterian churches, where the metrical Psalter was so universally used, the eighteenth-century introduction of Paraphrases (which included hymns which were not paraphrases) did not provoke any general controversy, and the idea of paraphrases was sanctioned by such evangelical leaders as Ralph Erskine whose own verses were widely sung.[22] Among the men in the forefront of the Free Church of Scotland after 1843, many are known to have believed that Christians were warranted to sing hymns of human composition. At the end of his life, the last books which William Cunningham asked for at his bedside were the *Confession of Faith* and *Olney Hymns*, and his farewell to colleagues was expressed in the words of a hymn.[23] Of the same mind, John Duncan wrote: 'Hymnologies are of great use; but we should have a better selection of hymns.'[24] For four months at the end of Thomas Guthrie's life, family members would sit with him through the night and 'beguile weariness . . . by softly singing a psalm or hymn.' 'Though I never composed music,' commented the eminent preacher, 'music has often composed me.'[25] When the aged Robert Candlish was told that the end was near, we read that he responded with the words:

[22] When his verse was based on Old Testament texts, Erskine defended his practice of importing into the text more than it actually contained as, in his words, 'adapting this paraphrase upon an Old Testament song to a New Testament dispensation.' *Works*, vol. 10, p. 316. Quoted by Annan, *Letters on Psalmody*, p. 86.

[23] Robert Rainy and James Mackenzie, *Life of William Cunningham* (London:Nelson, 1871), pp. 474–6.

[24] Duncan, *Colloquia Peripatetica*, ed. W.Knight (Edinburgh, 1907), p. 60.

[25] *Autobiography of Thomas Guthrie and Memoir*, D. K. Guthrie, vol. 2 (London: Daldy, 1875), pp. 473–4.

'Pray for me. I do not want deep experience, or great rapture, but just to rest on the facts that Christ died and that he is mine;' and then lifting his hand over his head, he said:

> *'Jesus, my Lord, I know His name;*
> *His name is all my boast;*
> *Nor will He put my soul to shame,*
> *Nor let my hope be lost.'*[26]

The words are those of Isaac Watts as found in the *Scottish Paraphrases*. Paraphrases were commonly sung in the Free Church and other Scottish Presbyterian Churches. R. L. Stevenson, who was brought up in the Free Church of the nineteenth century, once commented: 'The happiest lot on earth is to be born a Scotsman. You must pay for it in many ways, as for all other advantages on earth. You have to learn the *Paraphrases* and the *Shorter Catechism*.'

There was a Free Church of Scotland minority at this period who held to exclusive psalm-singing. But in defending their position they recognised the difficulty of asserting that paraphrases and hymns are prohibited in all circumstances, and claimed that the prohibition applies only to public worship. Thus John Kennedy said:

'Some desire them [hymns] because of an experience of enjoyment in using them, in private or in social Christian conference, to express their feeling of sorrow, hope, or gladness. Let these continue so to use them; I will yield to none in my desire to have them as a vehicle of any strong spiritual feeling that stirs my heart; but to use them in the worship of God in the sanctuary is quite another thing.'[27]

[26] Wilson, *Memorials of Candlish*, p. 590.
[27] *Proceedings and Debates of the General Assembly of the Free Church of Scotland*, 1872, p. 323.

But Dr Kennedy, and those who took his view, provided no evidence that there is a scriptural warrant for the distinction they wanted to draw. Does the praise commanded in one of the key New Testament texts, Ephesians 5:19, sound as though its directions belong to 'the sanctuary' or only to certain times – 'Giving thanks always for all things unto God' (5:20)?[28] Is the praise sung sincerely to God's glory in one place, or by an individual alone, an offence to God if it is sung in another place and by a congregation? Are hymns sung in private or in 'social Christian conference' not also directed to God or are they only to be valued for the 'experience of enjoyment'? It would appear that the inability of exclusive-psalm-singers to answer such questions contributed largely to the outcome of the debate in the Free Church of Scotland in 1872 which led to the provision of a full hymn book. It was not until early in the twentieth century that the Free Church of Scotland officially restricted all praise to the words of the metrical Psalter.[29]

[28] 'There are some people who seem to think that the Apostle is here laying down and prescribing church worship once and for ever, an order never to be varied. They regard this as almost a legal enactment prescribing the order of church worship. I think it is quite obvious from the context that it is not.' D. M. Lloyd-Jones, *The Westminster Record,* Sept. 1968, sermon on Ephesians 5:19 (repr. Southampton: Mayflower Christian Bookshop, n.d.), p. 130. This sermon sets out his reasons against exclusive psalmody. One metrical psalm was sung at Westminster Chapel every Sunday.

[29] This was a change against which J. Hay Thorburn protested in his pamphlet, *The Church of 1843 Dr Chalmers' Ideal, Versus a New Celtic Free Church* (Leith, 1908). The fullest discussion known to us on the whole psalms/hymns debate is to be found in the *Proceedings and Debates of the General Assembly of the Free Church of Scotland*, the volumes published between 1866 and 1872 (Edinburgh: James Nicol).

Certainly this discussion cannot be settled by an appeal to history but the idea that the highest standards of orthodoxy have ever been associated with 'psalms only' in praise has to be refuted. The quotations we have given are only intended to show that the argument that the most Reformed men and churches have held to a principle of exclusive psalmody is without foundation. William Annan went too far when he wrote in 1859, that the idea of the Psalter 'as the system of praise for the church in all ages, is purely a modern discovery.'[30] But the argument that the case against hymns was commonly accepted in the English-speaking churches before the nineteenth century cannot be sustained.[31]

THE POSITIVE CASE FOR HYMNS

I believe it can be argued from the New Testament not simply that the case for hymns is left open, but that there is good reason for believing that the praise of the church was not intended to be left precisely where it was in the former dispensation. Certainly, as claimed above, the Holy Spirit might have so indited the Psalms that additional praise would never be needed. Indeed he might have so composed the Old Testament that much of the New would never have needed to be written. The question is, Did he do so? Was the

[30] William Annan, *Letters on Psalmody: A Review of the Leading Arguments for the Exclusive Use of the Book of Psalms* (Philadelphia: Martien, 1859), p. 40.

[31] It is true that organised opposition to hymns could not precede their widespread introduction in the eighteenth century, but nineteenth-century exclusive-psalm-singing authors sought to argue as though the exclusive principle had always been accepted. Apart from John Cotton, 1650, I know of no writer defending that principle until William Romaine, *Works*, vol. 5 (London: Crosby, 1813).

Psalter intended as a part of the church's praise throughout the ages, or was it provided as the final and perfect manual of song?

The continuity between Old and New Testaments has often been an area of difference among Christians. It is certain that great injury has been done in the churches by those who place such a gulf between the Old and the New that the former virtually ceases to possess authority. True Christianity is built upon the whole Bible, not upon one Testament (2 *Tim.* 3:16–17). Contemporary low views of God in the churches are in no small measure connected with neglect of the Old Testament.

But while this must be granted, and emphasised, it is no less important to understand that the coming of Christ and his finished work ensured a great advance in light and privilege for the people of God. Reflecting on the magnitude of this difference, Stephen Charnock, the Puritan, wrote:

'Though God commanded love in the Old Testament, yet the manner of giving the law bespoke more of fear than love – Instead of the terrible voice of the law, Do this and live; the comfortable voice of the gospel is, Grace, Grace. Upon this account, the principle of the Old Testament was fear, and the worship often expressed by the fear of God; the principle of the New Testament is love. "The mount Sinai gendereth to bondage", Gal. 4:24; mount Zion, from whence the gospel or evangelical law goes forth, gendereth to liberty – and therefore the worship of God, under the gospel or New Testament, is oftener expressed by love than fear, as proceeding from higher principles, and acting nobler passions.'[32]

[32] Charnock, *Complete Works*, vol. 1(Edinburgh: Nichol, 1864), pp. 305–6.

Many texts indicate that, while regeneration and the way of salvation were the same in both testaments (*John* 3:10), a mighty change in spiritual experience was brought in by the coming of Christ.

'Among them that are born of women there hath not arisen a greater than John the Baptist: notwithstanding he that is least in the kingdom of heaven is greater than he' (*Matt.* 11:11). As David Brown says on that text: 'John stood on the very edge of the new economy, though belonging to the old: but for this very reason, the humblest member of the new economy was in advance of him.'[33]

'The Holy Ghost was not yet given; because Jesus was not yet glorified' (*John* 7:39).

'Hitherto ye have asked nothing in my name: ask, and ye shall receive, that your joy may be full' (*John* 16:24).

'The mystery of Christ which in other ages was not made known unto the sons of men, as it is now revealed unto his holy apostles and prophets by the Spirit' (*Eph.* 3:4–5).

I repeat, the difference between Old and New, and reflected by such texts, is relative and not absolute. But difference there is and it is closely related to matters which have much to do with the subject of praise. All evangelical truth can be found in the Psalter, but not to the degree in which it is now made known. The Holy Spirit was present in the Old Testament, but he was not then poured out. The day was coming when singing would move from Levitical choirs, and accompanying Temple ritual, to whole churches singing because 'filled with the Spirit' (*Eph.* 5:18–19). God was always the Father of his people but 'the Spirit of adoption, whereby we cry, Abba, Father' (*Rom.* 8:15) was

---

[33] Brown, *The Four Gospels* (repr. Edinburgh; Banner of Truth, 1976), p. 251. Further on this subject, see John Calvin, *Institutes*, ii.ix.

not the common possession of the church before the day which 'brought life and immortality to light through the gospel' (*2 Tim.* 1:10).

Is it then credible that the language of Christian praise must ever be confined to the words of an age of far less light and privilege? Is this difference between Old and New to be recognised in preaching and prayer but not in song?

By way of response, those who hold to exclusive psalmody say that the Christian is able to bring the full light of the New into his use of the Psalms. The gospel, it is said, is already there, for Jesus himself asserts it (*Luke* 24:44), and therefore we may sing with the understanding of those who enjoy the fulfilment of what the Spirit 'testified beforehand of the sufferings of Christ and the glory that should follow' (*1 Pet.* 1:11).

This may sound feasible but the fact is that it is difficult, and at times impossible, to make the language of David and Asaph the most appropriate expression of Christian experience. 'Can we believe this to be the best method of worshipping God,' asked Isaac Watts, 'to sing one thing and mean another? Besides that, the very literal sense of many of these expressions is exceeding deep and difficult, and not one in twenty of a religious assembly can possibly understand them at this distance from the Jewish days.'[34] Watts gives many instances from the Psalms to show that 'there are many hundreds of verses in that book which a

---

[34] 'An Essay for the Improvement of Psalmody', in *Works of Isaac Watts*, vol. 4 (London: Longman, 1753), pp. 279–80. His whole argument, although often attacked by exclusive-psalm-singers, is worthy of renewed attention. John Cotton conceded a difficulty in singing psalms but made a different deduction: 'To use the Psalms rightly . . . doth require a full and rich measure both of Spirit and Word to dwell in us.' *Singing of Psalms*, p. 20.

christian cannot properly assume without putting a very different meaning upon them.'[35]

Let us consider for a moment the subject at the centre of the gospel message, Christ crucified. By the inspiration of the Spirit psalmists wrote in places of Calvary, but they could not speak in such words as 'the Son of God loved me and gave himself for me'(*Gal*. 2:20). In Psalm 22 we see the cross of Christ, but to say that the words of that Psalm are all that the believer needs to sing about his Saviour's death is a strange deduction. A recent defender of exclusive psalmody has written: 'No human poet can advance beyond Psalm 22 or indeed approach anywhere near it.'[36] Such a statement confuses two different things. Our words to God are not required to be identical with his Word to us. The question, 'How can it be an improvement in church worship to substitute uninspired human compositions for the Word of God?' assumes no difference between revelation and response to that revelation. Psalm 22 is an inspired foreshadowing of Christ's sufferings. But it does not follow that because the Psalm is inspired, it has to be the most appropriate language we can use, standing

---

[35] Watts, *Essay*, p. 279. For examples he gives *Psa*. 68:13–16; 81:2–3; 84: 3–6; 108:2, 7–9; 58:8; 109; 134. A psalm-singing theologian of the stature of Patrick Fairbairn, while dealing with the subject of the imprecatory psalms, gives support to Watts' argument. He says that whereas the psalmist prayed for the destruction of enemies, Christians have to strive to 'subdue the corruption of ungodly men . . . to destroy them as enemies, in order that as friends they may pass over into the ranks of God's people . . . one may, indeed should, have respect to a change for the better in the spiritual relation of the parties concerned.' *The Revelation of Law in Scripture* (Edinburgh: Clark, 1869), pp. 362–3.

[36] Roy Mohon, *Make His Praise Glorious: A Defence of the Book of Psalms* (Eaglescliffe: WMP, 1999), p. 24.

as we do in the light of the fulfilment of prophecy. With reference to what we sing George Herbert is surely right when he says:

> *The fineness which a Hymn or Psalm affords*
> *Is when the soul unto the lines accords.*

So if the question is asked, whether Psalm 22 better expresses the feelings of the believer to Christ crucified than such hymns as, 'O Sacred Head! sore wounded'; 'And can it be that I should gain'; or, 'When I survey the wondrous cross'; we can surely say that it does not. And it does not because it was not intended to do so. The difference between psalmody and hymnody is greater still when it comes to the language of full assurance of salvation. If the words of Charnock quoted above are true, then it is at this point one would expect the best hymnody to supplement the Psalter to the greatest advantage, and this is what we find. Of course, the language of assurance is in the Psalms; we see it in Psalms 23 and 103 and there are bright glimpses in the closing words of such Psalms as the sixteenth and the seventy-third. But the note is occasional rather than pervasive. There are no sustained themes on heaven in the Psalter. The day of 'Now are we the sons of God' (*1 John* 3:2) had not yet come; more had to happen first, and when it did it was inevitable that believers would speak and sing of Christ's love and the certainty of a Father's house in language other than David's. It is not accidental that on the subject of heaven – 'to be with Christ which is far better'– hymns have excelled the Psalter. The characteristic of the best hymn-writers is that they have been enabled to express the high privileges of this dispensation and that is the very reason why their words have had such enduring appeal in the churches.[37]

The desire for heaven could not be a characteristic of the Psalms but it is abundantly found in hymns, as in David Dickson's lines:

> *Haste, my beloved, and remove*
> *These interposing days;*
> *Then shall my passions all be love,*
> *And all my powers be praise.*

It is sometimes said that they only speak of the insufficiency of the Psalter as a manual of praise who do not know it. But that is not the case. James Hamilton, for instance, a life-long psalm singer, had this to say to a friend who 'scruples to use anything in addition to the Psalms':

'I would ask, Does it never strike you as a strange test of spirituality, that you should sing on for fifty years without ever mentioning Immanuel, the Rock of Ages, the Lamb of God, the Resurrection and the Life? Is it not a strange token of growth in grace and in meetness for heaven, that you should have been singing all this time without having yet come to the name of Jesus? How would you like it if every sermon – or if even one – were constructed on the pattern of your habitual praise, and never once named the name that is above every other? And in all seriousness, will it do to leave it out? "Hitherto have ye asked nothing in my name", said the Lord Jesus to good men who up to that time had often said and sung the Psalms: "Ask, and ye shall receive." Both

[37] This is true of David Dickson, Richard Baxter and a multitude of successors. It is equally evident in the *Korean-English Hymnal* (Seoul: Korean Hymnal Society, 1984). The reunion of resurrected believers in glory is another aspect not evident in the Psalms.

prayers and praise need to be presented in Jesus' name; and whilst, blended with the new songs of our freer economy, the Psalms of David make the noblest substratum for Christian worship, they seem to ask for those Christian endings and New Testament doxologies which in our old and original Presbyterianism were attached to them.'[38]

I believe there is a confirmation from history of the argument that the larger blessings of the New Testament era warrant additional forms of praise. It is hardly accidental that the eras that have been richest in the production of scriptural hymns have been those when there has been a new measure of the Spirit given to the churches. Of course, it can be argued that corruptions and excesses have been produced in times of revival, but is that the most likely explanation why Luther, psalm-lover though he was, wrote so many hymns? Why the churches of the Great Awakening in America added hymns to their Psalms? Why the evangelical revival in England and Wales did the same? Why eminently-used preachers of the nineteenth century – Robert M'Cheyne,[39] Horatius Bonar, Asahel Nettleton, C. H. Spurgeon – all wrote hymns? Is it not far more in keeping with the New Testament to believe that when men and women are filled with the Spirit they will want to use words which reflect the Christian's larger privileges? Merle D'Aubigné, the historian of the Reformation, says that in the sixteenth century 'men could not confine themselves to

[38] Hamilton, *The Psalter and the Hymn Book*, pp. 16–17.

[39] 'He often rose a great while before it was day, and spent the time in prayer, and singing psalms and hymns, and the devotional reading of that Word which dwelt so richly in him.' 'Obituary Notice of the late Robert M'Cheyne', James Hamilton, *The Free Churchman*, Calcutta, 1843, p. 48.

mere translations of ancient hymns. The souls of Luther and many of his contemporaries . . . poured forth their feelings in religious songs . . . Thus the hymns were revived, which in the first century had consoled the pangs of the martyrs.'

There was reason for Louis Benson to say that the desire for the use of hymns 'arose from the fact that the canonical Psalms represented one dispensation and the worshippers another; and the difficulty was that of satisfying Christian devotion with the songs of an earlier stage of revelation.'[40]

Those who are committed to the exclusive use of the Psalms in public worship are generally far from thinking that they are being deprived of anything. Sometimes they speak as though 'purity of worship' was only known amongst them. They believe that the contrast in praise should not be drawn between Old and New Testaments but between inspired praise and mere human compositions. But if their case is wrong it is not hard to see that a level of experience more akin to the Old is liable to be the consequence. The present writer acknowledges that a few of the finest Christians he has known have been exclusive psalm singers: their lives and testimonies rose above the limitations of the language of their customary praise. That such is commonly the case in psalm-singing congregations is, however, as open to doubt today as it was in the time of Isaac Watts. In such congregations it is not normal for assurance of salvation to have the prominence which it ought to have, and the language of prayer can too easily become the language used 'before faith came' (*Gal.* 3:23). James Hamilton knew the psalm-singing churches of

[40] Benson, *The English Hymn*, p. 52. 'Chrysostom and Augustine both remark that to address God as "Father" is peculiar to the New Testament dispensation, and that the Old Testament sants never use the expression' (J. C. Ryle).

Scotland in one of their brightest eras, yet the danger to which I am referring was one of his arguments against the exclusive practice. 'It is a striking fact', he writes, 'that the prayers addressed to Christ in the Gospels are hardly one of them in Old Testament language.' But, he went on, the language of the Old tended to be too largely used by those who clung only to Psalms. This he illustrated by a story which had point because it was not singular. The child of a godly couple was sick and close to death. Although it was not the hour of family worship, the distraught mother 'prevailed on her husband to kneel down at the bed-side and "offer a word of prayer". The good man's prayer was chiefly taken from that best of liturgies, the book of Psalms, and after a long and reverential introduction from the 90th and elsewhere, he proceeded, "Lord, turn again the captivity of Zion: then shall our mouth be filled with laughter and our tongue with singing." And as he was proceeding, "Turn again our captivity," the poor agonised mother interrupted him, "Eh, man, you are aye drawn out for thae Jews; but it's our bairn that's deein" – at the same time clasping her hands and crying, "Lord, help us. Oh give us back our darling, if it be Thy holy will; and if he is to be taken, oh, take him to Thyself."'

'Fond as I am of scriptural phrases in prayer,' commented Hamilton, 'I am fonder still of reality.'[41]

POSTSCRIPT

It may be regretted that there should be any controversy on this subject, and regretted still more that in the past the difference has sometimes been discussed in a spirit unsuited to such a subject. But it might also be said to me:

[41] *The Psalter and the Hymn Book*, p. 14.

'Do we need any apologia for singing hymns today? Do the churches not rather need the vision of the majesty and holiness of God which is displayed in the Psalms? If you agree that Psalms are not wholly to be displaced (as they are in most places today), are you not emphasising the wrong thing?'

In reply, I agree Psalms are needed today. More psalm singing would be a blessing to many. But to urge the exclusive use of Psalms is the most likely way to discourage all hymn-singers from ever using a Psalter. The old Puritan phrase is relevant, 'Overdoing is undoing.' It is one thing to encourage the use of Psalms but quite another to teach that to use anything else is to depart from 'purity of worship'. And where that teaching goes in the name of loyalty to the Reformed Faith (as it sometimes does) it necessitates a response from those who believe that hymnody is an important part of our Christian heritage.

Conscientious disagreement may thus be unavoidable but all should agree that one thing is supremely necessary. Even the employment of the best manual of praise is no guarantee of true worship. As has been said, 'the mere language and music of praise is not praise'. Our first need is for a thankful heart and for the spirit of praise. And if song is intended to enliven and rouse our spirit then no outward means can make up for our spiritual failure. Too often the orthodox have given only secondary attention to the fact that music and song are the God-appointed means to raise the soul heavenwards. Calvin speaks of this when he writes:

'In truth, we know by experience that singing has great force and power to move and influence the heart of men to invoke and praise God with more vehement and ardent zeal . . . Among other things adapted for men's recreation and for giving them pleasure, music is either the foremost, or one of the principal; and we must esteem it as a gift designed for that purpose. Music has a secret and almost incredible power to move hearts.'[42]

Whatever our position, or our denomination, we can agree in the desire that our brief lives here be more truly lived to the praise of our Saviour. We know no better conclusion than the final words of an article on 'Psalmody of the Reformation':

'If heaven's bliss, as has been said, consists of love and song, – love the inner life, and song its outward expression, – let us seek, in the cultivation alike of the Christian grace and the sacred art, to prepare ourselves for the services of the upper sanctuary, where

"Ten thousand thousand are their tongues,
But all their joys are one."[43]

29 December 2000

---

[42] Quoted by Emil Doumergue, 'Music in the work of Calvin', *Princeton Theological Review*, October 1909, p. 536. To this should be added the observation of Robert Gossip, 'While the Romish idea of music had come to be, and still continues, that of an influence tending to awaken devotional sentiments in those who hear, the Reformers thought of it as the meet effect and expression of such sentiments already existing. Whatever came short of this was deemed contrary to the just conception of religious worship.' 'Metrical Versions of the Psalms', in the *Catholic Presbyterian,* vol. 2 (London: Nisbet, 1879), pp. 430–1.

[43] *British and Foreign Evangelical Review,* ed. William Cunningham (Edinburgh: Johnston and Hunter, 1854), pp. 125–6.

ADDITIONAL NOTES

Neither was it any objection against the psalmody of the church, that she sometimes made use of psalms and hymns of human composition, besides those of the sacred and inspired writers. St Austin [Augustine] himself made a psalm of many parts, in imitation of the 119th Psalm . . . there were always such psalms and hymns and doxologies composed by pious men and used in the church from the first foundation of it; nor did any but Paulus Samosatensis except against the use of them; which he did not because they were of human composition, but because they contained a doctrine contrary to his own private opinion. [A canon of the Council of Laodicea forbidding all 'private psalms'] was probably intended to exclude apocryphal psalms, or else such as were not approved by authority in the church. If it be extended further, it contradicts the current practice of the whole church . . . it is evident the ancients made no scruple of using psalms or hymns of human composition, provided they were pious and orthodox in substance, and composed by men of eminence, and received by just authority, and not brought clandestinely into the church.

JOSEPH BINGHAM, 'Of the Psalmody of the Ancient Church', *The Antiquities of the Christian Church* (1708–22, repr., vol. 2, London: H. G. Bohn, 1846), pp. 684–5.

David instituted the liturgical use of a few Psalms at least (e.g., 1 Chron.16:4ff.) . . . We are mistaken when we regard the entire Psalter as designed for the usage of the Temple. That some Psalms were so used cannot be denied, but it is interesting to note that liturgical directions are lacking for many of the Psalms. . . The Psalms in which the first person pronoun is employed are obviously designed to express primarily the experience of an individual. Of course, this does not preclude the usage of these Psalms in divine worship, but such usage is secondary. While today Christians should sing Psalms in the worship of the church, they do wrong to neglect the Psalter in individual devotions.

EDWARD J. YOUNG, *An Introduction to the Old Testament* (London: Tyndale Press, 1960), pp. 323–7.